THE DARK SIDE

CONFRONTING EVIL

JEREMIAH JOHNSTON

LifeWay Press® • Nashville, Tennessee

The Dark Side: Confronting Evil
Bible Studies for Life: Small Group Member Book

© 2017 LifeWay Press®

ISBN: 978-1-4627-4772-6
Item: 005794279

Dewey Decimal Classification Number: 235.4
Subject Heading: SPIRITUAL WARFARE \ DEVIL \ GOOD AND EVIL

Eric Geiger
Vice President, LifeWay Resources

Gena Rogers
Sam O'Neal
Content Editors

Michael Kelley
Director, Groups Ministry

Faith Whatley
Director, Adult Ministry

Send questions/comments to: Content Editor, *Bible Studies for Life: Adults*, One LifeWay Plaza, Nashville, TN 37234-0175; or make comments on the Web at BibleStudiesforLife.com.

Printed in the United States of America.

For ordering or inquiries, visit *lifeway.com*; write LifeWay Small Groups; One LifeWay Plaza; Nashville, TN 37234-0152; or call toll free (800) 458-2772.

We believe that the Bible has God for its author; salvation for its end; and truth, without any mixture of error, for its matter and that all Scripture is totally true and trustworthy. To review LifeWay's doctrinal guideline, please visit *lifeway.com/doctrinalguideline*.

All Scripture quotations, unless otherwise indicated, are taken from the the Christian Standard Bible®. Copyright 2017 by Holman Bible Publishers. Used by permission. The ESV® Bible (The Holy Bible, English Standard Version®) copyright © 2001 by Crossway, a publishing ministry of Good News Publishers. ESV® Text Edition: 2011. The ESV® text has been reproduced in cooperation with and by permission of Good News Publishers. Unauthorized reproduction of this publication is prohibited. All rights reserved.

Bible Studies for Life: Adults often lists websites that may be helpful to our readers. Our staff verifies each site's usefulness and appropriateness prior to publication. However, website content changes quickly so we encourage you to approach all websites with caution. Make sure sites are still appropriate before sharing them with students, friends, and family.

contents

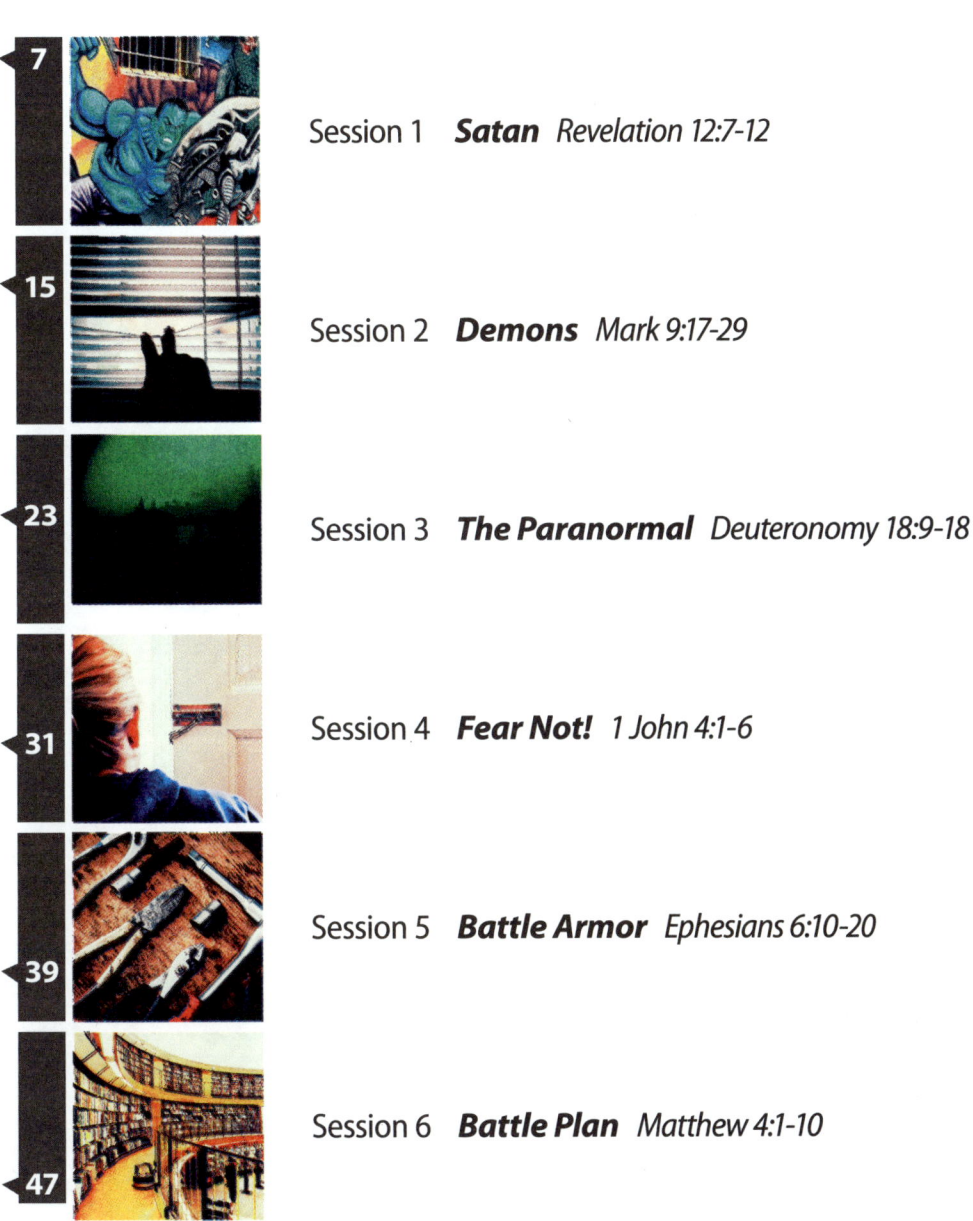

Session 1 **Satan** *Revelation 12:7-12*

Session 2 **Demons** *Mark 9:17-29*

Session 3 **The Paranormal** *Deuteronomy 18:9-18*

Session 4 **Fear Not!** *1 John 4:1-6*

Session 5 **Battle Armor** *Ephesians 6:10-20*

Session 6 **Battle Plan** *Matthew 4:1-10*

Leader Guide *page 58*

Social Media

Connect with a community of *Bible Studies for Life* users. Post responses to questions, share teaching ideas, and link to great blog content. **Facebook.com/BibleStudiesForLife**

Get instant updates about new articles, giveaways, and more. **@BibleMeetsLife**

The App

Bible Studies for Life is also available as an eBook. The eBook can be opened and read with the *Bible Studies for Life App*, a free app from the iOS App Store or the Google Play Store.

Blog

At **BibleStudiesForLife.com/blog** you will find additional resources for your study experience, including music downloads provided by LifeWay Worship. Plus, leaders and group members alike will benefit from the blog posts written for people in every life stage—singles, parents, boomers, and senior adults—as well as media clips, connections between our study topics, current events, and much more.

Training

For helps on how to use Bible Studies for Life, tips on how to better lead groups, or additional ideas for leading this session, visit: *ministrygrid.com/web/biblestudiesforlife.*

The battle is on. Join the fight!

Few people want to be in a battle. As followers of Christ, however, we're in the middle of a conflict that has been raging for thousands of years—whether we know it or not. Ours is a spiritual battle, and it's critical for us to know the stakes.

Anyone with military experience will tell you the value of knowing your enemy and determining what you're up against. In *The Screwtape Letters*, C. S. Lewis identified two wrong attitudes people often hold about evil: "There are two equal and opposite errors into which our race can fall about the devils. One is to disbelieve in their existence. The other is to believe, and to feel an excessive and unhealthy interest in them."[1]

In this study, *The Dark Side*, we'll take a deeper look at the truth about Satan, demons, and the pervasive evil in the paranormal world. Yes, those are dark subjects, but they're also critical for those of us who need to know what we're up against.

Thankfully, this study will also examine everything we've been given in Christ to stand against the forces of evil. We don't need to be afraid! In fact, through the truth of who we are in Christ and the armor He has made available to us, we can stand confidently against the devil's schemes.

Yes, Satan is mighty, but our God is Almighty!

Jeremiah J. Johnston

Jeremiah J. Johnston is Professor of Early Christianity at Houston Baptist University and President of the Christian Thinkers Society. He is the author of *Unanswered*. Jeremiah is married to Audrey, and they are parents to five children—including triplet boys! Follow Dr. Johnston on Twitter (@_jeremiah) and via the web at *ChristianThinkers.com*.

1. C. S. Lewis, *The Screwtape Letters* (New York: HarperOne, 2009) IX.

1 | SATAN

What monster or fictional villain best represents evil to you?

QUESTION #1

#BSFLdarkside

THE POINT

Satan fights against us, but we can stand in Christ.

THE BIBLE MEETS LIFE

We can't deny evil exists. It's all around us.

That reality struck home when I saw the shoes—piles of children's shoes. I was visiting the infamous Nazi concentration camp known as Buchenwald. Over 250,000 people were cruelly imprisoned there, and conservative estimates put the death toll between 40 and 50 thousand innocents. Seeing the ovens left little to the imagination, but it was the shoes of the countless children who died that hit me with the harsh reality of evil.

Unfortunately, evil isn't something we just see in fiction. Evil is no illusion, and while it can certainly reside in the hearts of people, such evil is most clearly seen in the one who seeks to inspire it: Satan. The Book of Revelation shows us exactly who this Satan is, the one who seeks to harm us.

Thankfully, the Book of Revelation also tells us of Satan's defeat. In this study, we'll see what Christ has done for us and how we can stand against Satan's schemes.

WHAT DOES THE BIBLE SAY?

Revelation 12:7-9

⁷ Then war broke out in heaven: Michael and his angels fought against the dragon. The dragon and his angels also fought, ⁸ but he could not prevail, and there was no place for them in heaven any longer. ⁹ So the great dragon was thrown out — the ancient serpent, who is called the devil and Satan, the one who deceives the whole world. He was thrown to earth, and his angels with him.

Revelation is a prophetic book full of visions and symbolism, which has given rise to a few disagreements in interpretation. Thankfully, John's apocalyptic vision is crystal clear about several key truths: God remains sovereign, He brings redemption to its complete fulfillment, and His eternal kingdom is firmly established. Revelation also reveals Christ as our victorious King.

Another truth that becomes clear in John's vision is Satan's defeat. Revelation 12 describes a war in which Satan, pictured as a great dragon, is defeated by God's angelic forces. When does this war take place? Some scholars believe the battle occurred at the time of Jesus' ascension, when the Son "was caught up to God and to his throne" (Rev. 12:5). Other scholars are convinced the battle will take place in the future—specifically, during the latter days of the tribulation.

We might differ on the timing of this war, but we can be clear on one thing: at its conclusion, Satan is defeated. Satan no longer has any right to be in heaven, the place where Jesus "has been exalted to the right hand of God" (Acts 2:33). But the devil doesn't go down without a fight. He still wants to destroy us.

Satan has been working to deceive God's people since the beginning. According to Jesus: "He was a murderer from the beginning and does not stand in the truth, because there is no truth in him. When he tells a lie, he speaks from his own nature, because he is a liar and the father of lies" (John 8:44).

> *What have you been taught about the devil?*
>
> **QUESTION #2**

BIBLE STUDIES FOR LIFE

THE POINT — *Satan fights against us, but we can stand in Christ.*

Make no mistake: Satan works to confuse us, lie to us, deceive us, and ruin our lives and spiritual vitality. He tries to get us to see things from our distorted human perspective rather than with our hearts devoted to the honor and glory of our Creator.

The unfortunate truth is that we believe the enemy's lies on a regular basis. He is crafty, and we are easy targets when we're unprepared. Therefore, followers of Christ must be ever vigilant. We must keep our focus on God and God's will rather than our own desires.

> *Where do you see evidence of Satan's deceptive work in the world today?*
>
> **QUESTION #3**

Revelation 12:10

¹⁰ **Then I heard a loud voice in heaven say, "The salvation and the power and the kingdom of our God and the authority of his Christ have now come, because the accuser of our brothers and sisters, who accuses them before our God day and night, has been thrown down.**

Did you know that "Devil" is not a personal name? Neither is "Satan." These are titles that describe our enemy's evil body of work. In the Greek language, the word *diabolos* refers to someone who slanders and accuses. The devil is continually speaking against us.

Indeed, we see in Revelation 12 that Satan not only seeks to deceive us, he also seeks to accuse us—just as he accused others throughout God's Word:

- ▶ **The devil accused Job.** Satan stood before God and accused the righteous Job of not having a deep commitment to God. He even accused God of protecting Job from harm so that the man would not reveal his true nature. (See Job 1:9-11.)

- ▶ **The devil accused Joshua.** Zechariah saw a vision in which Satan stood at the right side of the high priest, Joshua, to accuse him. (See Zech. 3:1.)

NOT EVEN CLOSE

People often view God and Satan as opposing forces of equal strength—good and evil locked in an eternal struggle. In reality, God is superior to Satan in every way. It's not even close. Use the chart below to list some of God's attributes, along with how Satan compares. (An example is provided.)

God	**Satan**
Omnipresent (He exists everywhere)	Exists only in one place at a time

How can the church better communicate the reality of God's superiority over Satan?

THE POINT — *Satan fights against us, but we can stand in Christ.*

▶ **The devil accuses us.** You surely have felt his accusations. *"You've sinned too much." "You're not good enough." "If you really loved Jesus, you wouldn't think that way." "You've failed."*

Satan is relentless; he desires to accuse us "before our God day and night." His accusations can sting, but let's not lose sight of a greater truth: this lying accuser has been thrown down.

Because of Christ, we have an Advocate—someone who stands with us against Satan's accusations.

▶ **The Lord stood with Joshua.** In Zechariah's vision, the Lord answered Satan's accusations by saying: "The Lord rebuke you, Satan! May the Lord who has chosen Jerusalem rebuke you!" (Zech. 3:2).

▶ **The Lord stood with Peter.** Hours before His arrest and trial, Jesus said to Peter, "Simon, Simon, look out. Satan has asked to sift you like wheat. But I have prayed for you that your faith may not fail" (Luke 22:31-32).

▶ **The Lord stands with us.** Satan was defeated through the work of Christ, and Christ now stands for us. He is our Advocate: "If anyone does sin, we have an advocate with the Father—Jesus Christ the righteous one" (1 John 2:1).

Believing Satan's lies can destroy our spiritual vitality. We must know our enemy's tactics, and we must always return to the reality of our faith and the forgiveness we've received through Jesus Christ.

> *How should we understand Satan's role as our "accuser"?*
>
> **QUESTION #4**

Revelation 12:11-12

¹¹ They conquered him by the blood of the Lamb and by the word of their testimony; for they did not love their lives to the point of death. ¹² Therefore rejoice, you heavens, and you who dwell in them! Woe to the earth and the sea, because the devil has come down to you with great fury, because he knows his time is short."

So far we've seen that Satan is relentless in his deceit and accusations. That can feel overwhelming when we remember how powerful he is. But don't lose heart! Satan may be powerful, but God is all-powerful. Satan is a created being with limitations. He is certainly no equal with God.

Best of all: *he is already defeated!*

One of the blessings of the gospel is that we don't have to bring about Satan's defeat; we only have to stand in the victory we receive through Jesus. Looking ahead to the cross, Jesus said: "Now is the judgment of this world. Now the ruler of this world will be cast out. As for me, if I am lifted up from the earth I will draw all people to myself" (John 12:31-32). Our victory is assured because, after He died, Jesus walked out of a borrowed tomb. Our redemption and our relationship with the Victor is eternally secure.

"Who can bring an accusation against God's elect? God is the one who justifies. Who is the one who condemns? Christ Jesus is the one who died, but even more, has been raised; he also is at the right hand of God and intercedes for us" (Rom. 8:33-34).

According to Revelation 12:12, Satan "knows his time is short." That's why he stays after us—and that's why we need to stay vigilant. Satan will attack, but we can resist him by daily lifting up Jesus in our lives and dying to our "old" selves. No more darkness; no more bondage. Jesus said: "I am the light of the world. Anyone who follows me will never walk in the darkness but will have the light of life" (John 8:12).

We can stand against Satan because we can stand in Christ.

> *What are some ways we can defend against Satan's accusations?*
>
> QUESTION #5

THE POINT — *Satan fights against us, but we can stand in Christ.*

LIVE IT OUT

We can overcome Satan through Jesus. What will you do this week to walk in that victory?

- ▶ **Confess.** Turn from sin and give Satan no grounds for accusations in your life. Place your trust in Christ for forgiveness and freedom.

- ▶ **Read.** Make Scripture reading a daily habit. Let the truth of Scripture fill your mind rather than the deceit and lies of Satan. Test every thought to see how it stands against the truth of Christ in His Word.

- ▶ **Speak.** When you see others living in false guilt because of Satan's lies, point to the victory they can have in Christ. Lead them to embrace the truth and walk in victory.

Don't fall into the trap of believing evil doesn't exist—or believing that evil only impacts the world in faraway places. Satan is a clear and present danger to God's people. Thankfully, our status as God's people means we can claim the victory He has already won.

My thoughts _____

Share with others how you will live out this study: **#BSFLdarkside**

2 | DEMONS

What do you typically do when you feel afraid?

QUESTION #1

#BSFLdarkside

THE POINT

Demonic forces are real, but Christ is greater.

THE BIBLE MEETS LIFE

Ever had a hex placed on you? How about a curse? I have.

My father is an evangelist. I was there the night his preaching was disrupted by a couple, all dressed in black, praying out loud to Satan. They were reciting the Lord's Prayer—backwards. It didn't stop there. I learned Satanists had been sending letters decorated with pentagrams to churches where my dad was preaching. We also learned the Satanists were putting hexes on our family.

I was afraid—but my dad wasn't. When I asked him about it, he said: "Son, truthfully, I was afraid at first. But Jesus is greater than any spiritual power, and He said He has given us all authority in Him to defeat the enemy."

Wow. That answer brought me peace because it proved to be true. In the Gospel of Mark, we read of another father and son facing demonic attack. They were also afraid. Yet, when Jesus entered the situation, the people became amazed and the demons trembled.

WHAT DOES THE BIBLE SAY?

Mark 9:17-22a

17 Someone from the crowd answered him, "Teacher, I brought my son to you. He has a spirit that makes him unable to speak. 18 Whenever it seizes him, it throws him down, and he foams at the mouth, grinds his teeth, and becomes rigid. I asked your disciples to drive it out, but they couldn't." 19 He replied to them, "You unbelieving generation, how long will I be with you? How long must I put up with you? Bring him to me." 20 So they brought the boy to him. When the spirit saw him, it immediately threw the boy into convulsions. He fell to the ground and rolled around, foaming at the mouth. 21 "How long has this been happening to him?" Jesus asked his father. "From childhood," he said. 22a "And many times it has thrown him into fire or water to destroy him."

In Mark 9:2-10, Jesus went up a high mountain with three of His disciples—Peter, James, and John—where He was transformed before them into His glorious appearance. When they came back down, they found a crowd gathered around a father and son. An evil spirit clearly had control of the boy, and the terrified father described how the spirit would often seize the child, forcing him to do terrible things.

Such an encounter would frighten most people, but surely not the disciples, right? They'd already seen Jesus exercise His authority over evil spirits. (See vv. 1-13.) Plus, under Jesus' authority, they themselves had cast out demons. (See 6:7-13.) But in this case, the disciples were powerless. We'll focus on their lack of power when we study Mark 9:28-29, but notice that Jesus called them an "unbelieving generation."

The apostles were powerless to help because of their lack of faith—but not Jesus. He was unfazed by the situation. Right in the middle of that desperate moment, Jesus offered the father and the gathered crowd the most welcoming of words: "Bring him to me."

> *What have you been taught about demons and demon possession?*
>
> QUESTION #2

THE POINT — *Demonic forces are real, but Christ is greater.*

Mark 9:22b-27

²²ᵇ "But if you can do anything, have compassion on us and help us." ²³ Jesus said to him, " 'If you can'? Everything is possible for the one who believes." ²⁴ Immediately the father of the boy cried out, "I do believe; help my unbelief!" ²⁵ When Jesus saw that a crowd was quickly gathering, he rebuked the unclean spirit, saying to it, "You mute and deaf spirit, I command you: Come out of him and never enter him again." ²⁶ Then it came out, shrieking and throwing him into terrible convulsions. The boy became like a corpse, so that many said, "He's dead." ²⁷ But Jesus, taking him by the hand, raised him, and he stood up.

It's easy for many of us to relate to the father in this encounter, since we've also felt defeated by the enemy at times and bewildered about what to do. In the quicksand of our experiences, we turn to Jesus. That's what this father did. His faith was pretty wimpy, but at least he was looking in the right direction.

Perhaps Jesus smiled when He heard the father's doubt: "If you can?" In other words: *Think about what you just said. Of course I can!* Jesus didn't criticize the man, but He did want the father to realize he had no reason for weak faith. Then the Lord uttered one of the most powerful sentences in the New Testament: "Everything is possible for the one who believes." Everything you do in life—relationships, marriage, family life, work, and decisions—will only be "successful" to the degree you are able to flex your muscle of faith and trust Almighty God. Our only escape from spiritual attack is through faith in a God who can do everything possible to come to our aid.

Unfortunately, Jesus' declaration is often misused. When people hear, "Everything is possible for the one who believes," they sometimes interpret that statement as a blanket promise that, if we just believe hard enough, we'll get whatever we ask for.

> *What strikes you as most interesting about these verses? Why?*
>
> **QUESTION #3**

Other Scriptures passages clarify the truth:

▶ "Whatever you ask in my name, I will do it so that the Father may be glorified in the Son. If you ask me anything in my name, I will do it" (John 14:13-14).

▶ "This is the confidence we have before him: If we ask anything according to his will, he hears us. And if we know that he hears whatever we ask, we know that we have what we have asked of him" (1 John 5:14-15).

God is not a genie in a bottle. As long as we are centered in Christ and His will, God will provide everything we need (i.e., all things will be possible for us). What does He ask of us? Faith. He will move the mountains in our lives, and He will remove us from spiritual bondage and confusion, but we must trust Him to do it.

In Mark 9, the issue wasn't Jesus' ability—He is all-powerful. Instead, the issue was the father's faith. To that end, the father responded to Jesus with one of the most transparent statements in the gospels: "I do believe; help my unbelief!"

The next moment is touching. After Jesus forced the demon out, the boy "became like a corpse." Jesus took the boy's hand and "raised him." That term, "raised him," is the same one used throughout the New Testament to speak of God raising Jesus from the dead. (See Acts 3:15; 4:10; 5:30; Eph. 1:20.) Our God, who raised Jesus from the dead, works powerfully to raise us out of our darkest situations.

> ***When have you felt like the father in these verses—wanting to believe but struggling to do so?***
>
> *QUESTION #4*

BIBLE STUDIES FOR LIFE

| THE POINT | *Demonic forces are real, but Christ is greater.* |

Mark 9:28-29

28 After he had gone into the house, his disciples asked him privately, "Why couldn't we drive it out?" **29** And he told them, "This kind can come out by nothing but prayer."

Jesus had helped the father with his faith; now He needed to help His disciples with theirs. In a private discussion, the disciples wanted to know why they'd failed. We should applaud their self-evaluation, but in their introspection they were still looking at themselves. "Why couldn't *we* drive it out?" (emphasis added). Their mistake was in looking only at their own abilities and strength.

Just like the boy's father, the disciples also needed to continually exercise faith. They had failed to match up with the enemy because they failed to trust in and depend on God.

When Jesus said, "This kind can come out by nothing but prayer," He wasn't making a distinction—as though only certain demons require prayer to cast them out, but others don't. The truth is that *whenever* we engage in spiritual battle, we need to pray and express our faith in the One with all the power. (See Eph. 6:18.) Only prayer moves us from relying on our strengths (which are actually weaknesses) to trusting the all-powerful God who desires to set us free and has the power to do so.

Prayer is an expression of our total dependence upon God; it shows we need God's intervention in something we can't do on our own. Prayer is indispensable in spiritual warfare, and our faith is strengthened when we pray earnestly. It's in response to prayer that God unleashes "the immeasurable greatness of his power toward us who believe, according to the mighty working of his strength" (Eph. 1:19).

Unfortunately, many Christians are not aware of their authority in Jesus Christ, which means we often lack confidence to stand against spiritual attacks. We'll study in a later session the armor God has given us to stand and engage in battle, but let's note for the moment that any confidence we have to stand against the enemy is not self-confidence; it's confidence in Jesus Christ—the One with all power and authority on whom we totally depend.

> *Why is faith in Jesus essential when dealing with evil?*
>
> QUESTION #5

PERSONAL ASSESSMENT: PRAYER

Prayer is a critical tool in our battle against evil. Use the following questions to get a sense of how deeply your prayers reflect your faith in God.

Do you pray primarily during moments of crisis, or do you pray regularly throughout each day?

1   2   3   4   5   6   7   8   9   10

(Crisis)   (Regularly)

Do you pray primarily for your will to be accomplished, or for God's will?

1   2   3   4   5   6   7   8   9   10

(Your will)   (God's will)

How often do you express your trust and confidence in God's authority?

1   2   3   4   5   6   7   8   9   10

(Rarely)   (Regularly)

THE POINT — *Demonic forces are real, but Christ is greater.*

LIVE IT OUT

What steps can you take to ground yourself in Christ as preparation for the enemy's attacks? Consider the following suggestions:

- ▶ **Pray often.** Ask God to increase and strengthen your faith. Make it a habit to ask God to strengthen your faith and guide you into a deeper truth in Him.

- ▶ **Pray daily.** Stop relying on yourself as you face difficulties and spiritual attacks. Express your total dependence on God through prayer at the beginning of each day.

- ▶ **Pray constantly.** Invite the presence of Jesus into every situation. Form the discipline of continually conversing with God's Spirit as you encounter new situations and circumstances throughout each day.

As disciples of Jesus, we don't need to look for a "demon under every bush"—but neither should we be unaware or unprepared. Use prayer to keep yourself intimately connected with God's power through Jesus Christ.

My *thoughts*

Share with others how you will live out this study: **#BSFLdarkside**

3 | THE PARANORMAL

What movies or TV shows bank on our culture's interest in the paranormal?

QUESTION #1

#BSFLdarkside

BIBLE STUDIES FOR LIFE   23

THE POINT

Dabbling with evil is destructive; seeking direction from God brings life.

THE BIBLE MEETS LIFE

Everyone's heard of ghost stories. In fact, among Americans:

- 71 percent claim to have had a paranormal experience.
- 34 percent believe in ghosts.
- 56 percent believe ghosts are spirits of the dead.
- 37 percent believe houses can be haunted.
- 55 percent believe psychics have real power.[1]

Even many of those who don't "believe" in ghosts still think it can be fun to play with the paranormal. That's a problem, because the paranormal is a slippery slope. Once a person gets curious and opens the door to the paranormal world, they only find trouble—and once opened, that door can be difficult to close.

How can we escape the appeal of these dangers? Moses, the great lawgiver, provided us with a helpful road map for avoiding the dangerous pitfalls of the paranormal.

WHAT DOES THE BIBLE SAY?

Deuteronomy 18:9-11

⁹ "When you enter the land the Lord your God is giving you, do not imitate the detestable customs of those nations. ¹⁰ No one among you is to sacrifice his son or daughter in the fire, practice divination, tell fortunes, interpret omens, practice sorcery, ¹¹ cast spells, consult a medium or a spiritist, or inquire of the dead."

Interest in the paranormal may seem trendy at the moment, but it's nothing new. God's people have been dealing with it literally for thousands of years. Indeed, one of the reasons God removed the Canaanites from the promised land was because of their spiritual darkness.

God wanted His people to be warned and prepared before they entered that promised land. Therefore, Moses identified several paranormal practices that were common among the pagans:

- ▶ **Child sacrifice.** Children were killed in order to appease a pagan god and influence events that god supposedly controlled. This was merely a cultural euphemism for child extermination.

- ▶ **Divination.** This was a general term for trying to gain insights from the gods through various means, including other practices listed in this passage.

- ▶ **Fortune telling.** While the Hebrew word used here is hard to define with certainty, it literally means "those who cause to appear." It might have referred to making apparitions appear or making a person's course of action visible through occultic practices.

- ▶ **Interpreting omens.** Those who practiced this sought to determine the future through the use of objects. For example, a diviner might have attempted to interpret the future based on how objects fell out of a cup.

> *What have you been taught about the practices mentioned in these verses?*
>
> QUESTION #2

BIBLE STUDIES FOR LIFE

THE POINT — *Dabbling with evil is destructive; seeking direction from God brings life.*

- **Sorcery.** Witches and sorcerers attempted to manipulate the powers of nature. Today we often refer to those who practice "black magic" in a similar way.

- **Casting spells.** The Hebrew term has the sense of binding or fascinating; it meant to bind a person with a curse.

- **Consulting the dead.** Moses used several terms—"medium," "spiritist," those who "inquire of the dead"—that each address attempting to communicate with the dead.

Though the distinction between these practices might seem minor, the combined list makes it abundantly clear: God considers "detestable" any form of divination, the occult, and paranormal practices. No matter how popular or profitable such practices may appear, we are never to "imitate" them.

> *Why do people still dabble in these kinds of practices?*
>
> **QUESTION #3**

Deuteronomy 18:12-14

12 "Everyone who does these acts is detestable to the Lord, and the Lord your God is driving out the nations before you because of these detestable acts. 13 You must be blameless before the Lord your God. 14 Though these nations you are about to drive out listen to fortune-tellers and diviners, the Lord your God has not permitted you to do this."

It's worth repeating: nothing good comes from dabbling in the paranormal. Yet studies show that almost one-third of Americans have consulted their horoscopes. Nearly 12 percent of Americans (roughly 42 million people) have personally consulted a psychic, medium, or fortune-teller. And nearly 25 percent of Americans like to research ghosts and haunted houses.[2]

The Bible's teaching is clear: "You must be blameless before the Lord your God." Not only that, but "Everyone who does these acts is detestable to the Lord."

26 SESSION 3

To be "blameless" doesn't mean we live in sinless perfection. Rather, we're blameless when we live with hearts fully committed to God—when we reflect His integrity and display an undivided heart committed to Him. David used the same Hebrew word in Psalm 101:2 when he wrote: "I will live with a heart of integrity in my house."

Notice there's no gray area or middle ground. Paranormal practices are in absolute conflict with pure devotion and worship of Yahweh—the One true God and the Creator of all. Therefore, if we're looking into any of the activities condemned in Deuteronomy 18, we're not looking toward God.

And when we fail to look to God, we will not be held blameless.

God's condemnation of these practices did not apply only to those in the Old Testament. The New Testament also commands followers of Jesus to avoid all interaction with the paranormal world:

- "Stay away from every kind of evil" (1 Thess. 5:22).
- "But have nothing to do with pointless and silly myths. Rather, train yourself in godliness" (1 Tim. 4:7).

As we'll see in the next portion of Deuteronomy 18, there's another reason why we should stay away from the paranormal: God has given us something far superior.

> **What makes paranormal practices so dangerous and destructive?**
>
> QUESTION #4

THE POINT — *Dabbling with evil is destructive; seeking direction from God brings life.*

WHAT WOULD YOU SAY?

People use a lot of excuses to rationalize dabbling in different paranormal activities. How would you respond if a close friend or family members used the excuses below? Choose one and respond.

"Reading my horoscope helps me get a sense of what I might encounter each day. It's just a little extra information."

"A group of people at the party wanted to use a Ouija Board, so I joined them. It wasn't a big deal."

"I went to the psychic because I was worried about Mom. I wanted to make sure she was in a good place after the accident."

How can the situation you addressed above become an opportunity to proclaim the truth of the gospel?

Deuteronomy 18:15-18

15 "The LORD your God will raise up for you a prophet like me from among your own brothers. You must listen to him. 16 This is what you requested from the LORD your God at Horeb on the day of the assembly when you said, 'Let us not continue to hear the voice of the LORD our God or see this great fire any longer, so that we will not die!' 17 Then the LORD said to me, 'They have spoken well. 18 I will raise up for them a prophet like you from among their brothers. I will put my words in his mouth, and he will tell them everything I command him.'"

At first glance, it might appear as if Moses abruptly changed subjects in verse 15. Actually, he was right on message. The pagans were using paranormal practices to seek divine guidance, determine the future, or manipulate events in their favor. Moses was pointing to something better for God's people.

In the place of pagan paranormal activity, Moses promised that God would raise up a new order of prophets who would reveal God's words to His people. He was speaking of more than just Deborah, Samuel, Elijah, Isaiah, Jeremiah, and the other prophets of the Old Testament. Moses was also pointing forward to the coming Redeemer—the Messiah, Jesus Christ. When Peter and Stephen preached to their fellow Jews about Jesus, they both used this same passage to point to Jesus as the supreme Prophet. (See Acts 3:22-23; 7:37.)

God spoke clearly through His prophets, but one Prophet gave the ultimate word from God, because He is the ultimate Word of God. As the author of Hebrews wrote: "Long ago God spoke to the fathers by the prophets at different times and in different ways. In these last days, he has spoken to us by his Son. God has appointed him heir of all things and made the universe through him" (Heb. 1:1-2).

As I've counseled hurting people, I've discovered that those who turn to the paranormal world for help don't find the answers they seek. In fact, they find the opposite: depression, abuse, and even suicide. Jesus is a much better answer to our spiritual questions—and He offers a far greater hope.

> *What are reliable ways for us to seek out God's plan and purpose in our lives?*
>
> **QUESTION #5**

THE POINT — *Dabbling with evil is destructive; seeking direction from God brings life.*

LIVE IT OUT

What steps can you take this week to shine the light of Jesus against the darkness of the paranormal? Consider these suggestions:

- ▶ **Be educated.** You will only know God's guidance as you immerse yourself in His Word. Commit to reading the Bible on a daily basis and develop the practice of studying its truth.

- ▶ **Be discerning.** Make discernment a regular part of your prayer life. Ask God to guide your thoughts and actions away from evil. "But test all things. Hold on to what is good. Stay away from every kind of evil" (1 Thess. 5:21-22).

- ▶ **Be blameless.** Seek to demonstrate a blameless heart, fully devoted to the Lord, by removing from your presence anything that promotes and encourages the use of paranormal practices. Make a line in the sand.

People in our culture are fascinated with the paranormal because they are longing for God. Choose the path of light over darkness—not only for yourself, but for those who need to see Christ.

My thoughts

---

1. "Americans' Beliefs in Paranormal Phenomena" (Infographic) *LiveScience* [online] 28 October 2011 [cited 28 October 2016] Available from the Internet: *livescience.com/16748-americans-beliefs-paranormal-infographic.html*.
2. Christopher Bader, Carson Mencken, and Joseph Baker, *Paranormal America* (New York: New York University Press, 2010), 73, 107.

Share with others how you will live out this study: **#BSFLdarkside**

4 | FEAR NOT!

What are some of the most unusual phobias you've heard about?

QUESTION #1

#BSFLdarkside

BIBLE STUDIES FOR LIFE

THE POINT

We don't need to fear evil forces when we're in Christ.

THE BIBLE MEETS LIFE

She missed over 10,000 sunsets.

For nearly 30 years, Marjorie Goff never left her apartment. She suffered from severe agoraphobia, an anxiety disorder in which a person fears open spaces and crowds. Driven by fear, Marjorie created a self-imposed prison out of her apartment. Only after a caring friend patiently coaxed her into therapy did Marjorie experience the beauty of the outdoors again.[1]

Marjorie found freedom and healing when she accepted the truth. She stopped believing the lie about herself and her circumstances. She acted on the truth and stepped outside.

We all know what it is to fear. And when we consider the evil in the world, we can truly feel afraid. Satan and the spiritual forces of darkness are real. They seek to do us harm. That's scary.

Fortunately, as we'll see in 1 John 4:1-6, Christians need not fear the work of Satan or demons, because the One in us is greater than the one in the world.

WHAT DOES THE BIBLE SAY?

1 John 4:1-3

1 Dear friends, do not believe every spirit, but test the spirits to see if they are from God, because many false prophets have gone out into the world. 2 This is how you know the Spirit of God: Every spirit that confesses that Jesus Christ has come in the flesh is from God, 3 but every spirit that does not confess Jesus is not from God. This is the spirit of the antichrist, which you have heard is coming; even now it is already in the world.

Because God's people encountered false prophets in the Old Testament, God revealed two standards through Moses that enabled His people to distinguish between true and false prophets:

1. If a prophet announced a special sign or wonder that came true and then encouraged the people to follow other gods, he was a false prophet. (See Deut. 13:1-5.) True teaching never steers us away from the one, true God.

2. If a prophet announced something that did not come true, he was a false prophet. (See 18:22.) God is all-powerful and cannot lie, so His words will always come true. No exceptions.

Many centuries later, the apostle John was still dealing with false teachers—this time as a leader in the early church. "Do not believe every spirit," John wrote, "but test the spirits to see if they are from God."

Satan had updated his tactics at the launch of the church to include distortions of the truth about Jesus Christ. That's because Christianity rises or falls based on what we believe—and what we teach others—about Jesus.

John gave us a Christ-centered test by which to evaluate a person's beliefs and teaching. Stated simply: "Every spirit that confesses that Jesus Christ has come in the flesh is from God."

> *Who comes to mind when you hear the word "discernment"? Why?*
>
> **QUESTION #2**

THE POINT — *We don't need to fear evil forces when we're in Christ.*

There are two key elements to this test:

- **The full humanity of Jesus Christ is affirmed.** Note the emphasis on the phrase "come in the flesh." Christ was not a spirit being; He was a human being. John used the name given at His birth: Jesus. He was fully a man.

- **The full divinity of Jesus Christ is affirmed.** John also used the title given to Jesus: Christ. He is the Anointed One from God, the Messiah. He is God.

The Jesus revealed in the Gospels is clearly the Son of God who lived among the Jews, was crucified, and died a real death. Jesus also experienced a physical resurrection on the third day after His crucifixion. This resurrection confirmed everything He taught and showed that His life and death were approved by God.

Therefore, when you want to test the validity of a group, find out what that group teaches about Jesus. For example:

- **Mormonism** teaches that Jesus was the first spirit-child born to humanity's heavenly parents.

- **Jehovah's Witnesses** teach that Jesus was a spirit-creature created by God who later came to earth as a man.

- **Islam** teaches that Jesus was a highly revered prophet, but He was not the Son of God.

- **Hinduism** teaches that Jesus was a man who reached "god-consciousness."

The Scriptures are clear: *Jesus is both fully human and fully God.* Any religion, philosophy, or individual that rejects that foundational truth did not originate with God.

Satan is a master at corrupting the truth. But when we remain discerning and keep our eyes open by continually testing what we see and hear against God's Word, we will not be caught in error.

> *What are some distortions of the nature of Jesus we still hear today?*
>
> **QUESTION #3**

ALWAYS

Listen to the song "Always" by Kristian Stanfill. As you listen, record your thoughts on the following questions:

What comes to mind when the song references "foes," "storms," and "war"?

What comes to mind when the song references help coming from the Lord?

What emotions do you experience when you hear this song?

> "If God declares that all is well, ten thousand devils may declare it to be ill, but we laugh them all to scorn."
>
> — CHARLES SPURGEON

THE POINT	We don't need to fear evil forces when we're in Christ.

1 John 4:4-6

⁴ You are from God, little children, and you have conquered them, because the one who is in you is greater than the one who is in the world. ⁵ They are from the world. Therefore what they say is from the world, and the world listens to them. ⁶ We are from God. Anyone who knows God listens to us; anyone who is not from God does not listen to us. This is how we know the Spirit of truth and the spirit of deception.

> *What emotions do you experience when you read this passage?*
>
> **QUESTION #4**

So far in this study, we've seen what Scripture says about the evil work of Satan, demonic forces, and paranormal practices. The "dark side" truly is dark. Indeed, Christians may look at the different enemies arrayed against us and think, *What chance do we have?*

Thankfully, John reminded us of two great truths in verses 4-6.

First, you are from God. Believers—those who have a relationship with Jesus Christ—are brought into God's family. Therefore, we are secure in Him:

▶ "I give them eternal life, and they will never perish. No one will snatch them out of my hand. My Father, who has given them to me, is greater than all. No one is able to snatch them out of the Father's hand" (John 10:28-29).

▶ "For I am persuaded that neither death nor life, nor angels nor rulers, nor things present nor things to come, nor powers, nor height nor depth, nor any other created thing will be able to separate us from the love of God that is in Christ Jesus our Lord" (Rom. 8:38-39).

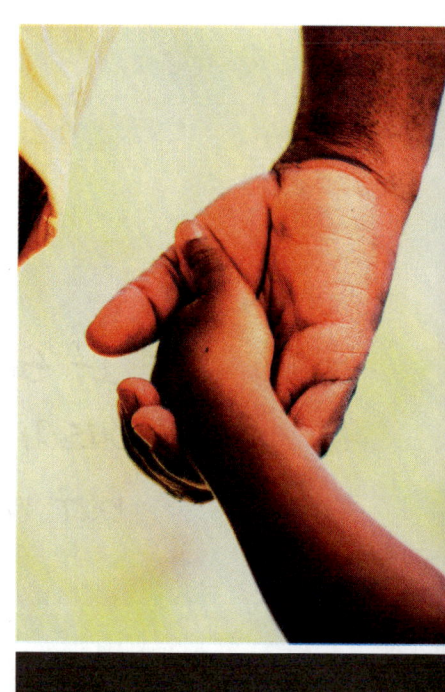

Second, you have conquered those who have the spirit of the antichrist. Our relationship with God is not just a secure, defensive position; it's an offensive position. We don't conquer evil by cowering in a corner. Because we are in Christ, we can boldly step out, test the spirits, and represent Christ in the face of any and all evil we encounter.

Of course, we don't conquer in our own power. Because we are from God and rest in Him, He has given us His own Holy Spirit. And it's only through the presence and power of that Spirit that we can conquer. At the moment we trust Christ as our Redeemer and Lord, the Holy Spirit indwells us.

A relationship with Christ and the powerful presence of the Holy Spirit go hand in hand:

- "If anyone does not have the Spirit of Christ, he does not belong to him" (Rom. 8:9).
- "Don't you know that your body is a temple of the Holy Spirit who is in you, whom you have from God?" (1 Cor. 6:19).

John reminded us about the incredible difference the Holy Spirit makes when facing the forces of Satan that oppose Christ: "The one who is in you is greater than the one who is in the world." Satan may be powerful, but God's Holy Spirit is infinitely more powerful. The false teachers and false prophets may sound wise, but our God's wisdom is boundless. The world can have great pull and persuasion, but the indwelling Spirit is immeasurably greater.

When we live under the lordship of God, leaning on Him and filled with His Spirit (see Eph. 5:18), He helps us to test the spirits we encounter. We don't need to fear being deceived by a powerful enemy. Why? Because we're resting in a greater power: the indwelling Holy Spirit who enables us to "know the Spirit of truth and the spirit of deception."

In Christ, we're placed in a great position to recognize evil and falsehood—and to stand against it. We truly have nothing to fear.

> *Jesus is greater than those who oppose us. How will this truth influence your life today and in the days to come?*
>
> QUESTION #5

THE POINT — *We don't need to fear evil forces when we're in Christ.*

LIVE IT OUT

How will the truth that you have nothing to fear in Christ make a difference in your life this week? Consider these suggestions:

> **Memorize.** If you're prone to fear, memorize 1 John 4:4. Place cards with this verse in various places where you will see them throughout the day. Recite it whenever you feel afraid.

> **Be filled.** God has placed His Holy Spirit in your life. Stay focused in prayer so you can continually rely on that Spirit to fill you, lead you, and give you discernment.

> **Be discerning.** Regularly evaluate the different "voices" you encounter in books, sermons, studies, online devotions, and articles. Determine what they believe about Christ and to what degree they lift up and honor the name of Christ.

Severe phobias aren't the only factor that keeps us from experiencing the life we were meant to live. Yes, evil is real. But so is God—and He is far superior to any force or opposition that might move against us. So don't be afraid!

My thoughts

---

1. Stephanie Mansfield, "For 30 Years She Was a Prisoner of Fear," *The Washington Post* [online], 25 October 1981 [cited 17 November 2016] Available on the Internet: *washingtonpost.com/archive/lifestyle/1981/10/25/for-30-years-she-was-a-prisoner-of-fear/5e69da62-eafc-4b06-88af-2952671912ae/*

Share with others how you will live out this study: **#BSFLdarkside**

5 BATTLE ARMOR

What are some "tools of the trade" you rely on most days?

QUESTION #1

#BSFLdarkside

THE POINT

God equips us for the spiritual battles we face.

THE BIBLE MEETS LIFE

The TV character MacGyver is known for his uncanny ability to get out of harrowing circumstances with mundane objects. Whether he's defusing a bomb, rescuing people, or escaping from a deadly trap, all MacGyver needs to save the day is his knowledge of science, a few paper clips, and some chewing gum.

Of course, the show is pure fiction. But sometimes it would be nice if we could save ourselves from life's problems and attacks by quickly grabbing whatever is at hand and creatively crafting tools to free ourselves. Right?

Thankfully, God has given us all we need to do just that. He's equipped us with the tools we need to stand strong in the face of attacks that come against us. Better than any tool we can create on our own, God has given us spiritual armor and weapons.

Yes, life is often a battle with Satan coming against us. But we are guaranteed victory when we trust in Christ and in the tools He has provided.

WHAT DOES THE BIBLE SAY?

Ephesians 6:10-13

¹⁰ Finally, be strengthened by the Lord and by his vast strength. ¹¹ Put on the full armor of God so that you can stand against the schemes of the devil. ¹² For our struggle is not against flesh and blood, but against the rulers, against the authorities, against the cosmic powers of this darkness, against evil, spiritual forces in the heavens. ¹³ For this reason take up the full armor of God, so that you may be able to resist in the evil day, and having prepared everything, to take your stand.

Jesus never promised the Christian life would be easy. Life by itself can be full of difficulties, but that difficulty is compounded by an enemy who is "prowling around like a roaring lion, looking for anyone he can devour" (1 Pet. 5:8). Therefore, Paul called us to "be strengthened by the Lord and by his vast strength." Our own strength is insufficient! This call to embrace the strength God gives echoes His words to Joshua: "Be strong and very courageous" (Josh. 1:7).

We, too, must embrace that same trust in God's strength if we hope to live the Christian life victoriously. But we're not in a battle to gain victory; we're strengthened in the Lord and we engage in spiritual warfare from a position of victory. The victory over Satan was won on the cross. Still, though Christ has defeated our enemy (see Rev. 12:10-11), defeated enemies don't always give up easily. When an enemy has nothing more to lose, he can even attack with greater intensity.

Paul reminded us why we need the Lord's strength: we face a powerful adversary who attacks strategically. Paul referred to "the schemes of the devil." Satan knows where, when, and how to target each of us. Our enemy is also organized; he works against us through his army: "the rulers, against the authorities, against the cosmic powers of this darkness, against evil, spiritual forces in the heavens."

What have you been taught about spiritual warfare?

QUESTION #2

THE POINT — *God equips us for the spiritual battles we face.*

Yes, we have victory in Christ. But Paul still called the battle we face a "struggle." The Greek word is actually tied to the sport of wrestling, which reminds us that we don't battle the spiritual forces of evil from a distance. Our fight is a close, hand-to-hand type of struggle—only we're not struggling in a physical context. Our fight is not "against flesh and blood." It's supernatural.

So how do we take on these evil forces that seek to harm us? We stand. In a position of Christ-centered confidence, Paul told us to "take your stand." We do that when we "take up the full armor of God." By doing so, we become active participants, not passive observers, in dealing with spiritual attack.

Ephesians 6:14-17

14 Stand, therefore, with truth like a belt around your waist, righteousness like armor on your chest, 15 and your feet sandaled with readiness for the gospel of peace. 16 In every situation take up the shield of faith with which you can extinguish all the flaming arrows of the evil one. 17 Take the helmet of salvation and the sword of the Spirit — which is the word of God.

God provides His armor for the battles we face in His name:

1. **Belt of truth.** The belt secured the rest of the soldier's armor and held his weapons. Truth is the belt of preparation for the believer. Everything we do is held in place when we accept and trust in God's Word.

2. **Breastplate of righteousness.** A soldier's breastplate covered the chest and protected the vital organs from arrows. Paul wasn't referring to our righteousness in Christ, which can never be taken away. Instead, he was referring

> *Which piece of God's armor most resonates with you? Why?*
>
> **QUESTION #3**

42 SESSION 5

to living in righteousness (see Eph. 4:24; 5:8-9)—our daily walk with Christ. The way we live protects us against spiritual attacks.

3. **Feet sandaled with readiness.** Roman soldiers were issued quality footwear: studded boots that allowed them to travel great distances and yet stand firmly in the heat of battle. We can stand firm or move forward because of His gospel of peace. Our standing is secure because of what Christ has done for us.

4. **Shield of faith.** A company of soldiers could interlock their shields and form a solid wall as they moved forward. Our shield is comprised of our faith—our trust in the promises and power of God. The enemy can fire his arrows of lies, doubts, accusations, and temptations at us, but our faith in God keeps us from falling prey to such attacks.

5. **Helmet of salvation.** A soldier protected his head with a heavy helmet of metal. Our helmet is our hope in Christ, which rests in the future we have in Him. Because of that hope, we refuse to succumb to the standards of this world.

6. **Sword of the Spirit.** The soldier's sword was short, like a dagger, and used for close combat. Our sword is God's Word; it's our only weapon that is both offensive and defensive. We rest in its promises to defend us, and we apply Scripture to specific situations to resist the enemy's attacks and send him running. (See Matt. 4:1-11.)

What are some real-life situations in which this armor is essential for followers of Christ?

QUESTION #4

BIBLE STUDIES FOR LIFE 43

THE POINT — *God equips us for the spiritual battles we face.*

Ephesians 6:18-20

18 Pray at all times in the Spirit with every prayer and request, and stay alert with all perseverance and intercession for all the saints. 19 Pray also for me, that the message may be given to me when I open my mouth to make known with boldness the mystery of the gospel. 20 For this I am an ambassador in chains. Pray that I might be bold enough to speak about it as I should.

We have one more tool at our disposal as we engage in spiritual battle: prayer. God has supplied us with all we need to stand, but we never stand alone. We need constant communication with the One we serve.

Prayer is more than mere *communication* with God; it's our *communion* with Him. Prayer is taking the promises of God and speaking them back to Him. It's a continual dependence upon Christ. We are to do this "at all times." Paul told the Thessalonians that Christians are to "pray constantly" (1 Thess. 5:17). Even as we're working, playing, and going about our daily routine, we are to be praying.

Why should we pray continually? Because we're in a battle. Soldiers know they can't slack off; they must remain vigilant. Paul called us to "stay alert with all perseverance and intercession for all the saints." We pray continually, ever alert to the attacks of the devil. But we don't just pray for ourselves; we pray "for all the saints." We pray for the strength of our fellow believers in this shared battle against evil. We also pray "in the Spirit with every prayer and request." As we pray for others and ourselves, we include praise, worship, thanksgiving, and confession—in addition to the requests we lay before God.

Notice that Paul made prayer personal. He said, "Pray also for me." Paul, the great apostle and evangelist, asked others to pray that he "might be bold enough to speak" the gospel. Paul knew any boldness he had came from God, and he was well aware of his need to remain dependent on Him.

We need boldness, too. Fortunately, the same Source that provided Paul's boldness sustains us, as well. We can move forward in the boldness Christ freely offers. But make no mistake: we cannot be bold for God until we have been bold with God in prayer.

> *How does prayer contribute to our efforts in spiritual warfare?*
>
> **QUESTION #5**

STANDING FIRM

What does it look like to stand firm against the spiritual forces of evil? Choose the image that best represents your understanding of what it means to stand firm. Or, use the blank box to draw your own image.

Who comes to mind as an example of someone who has taken a firm stand against the spiritual forces of evil? Why?

THE POINT *God equips us for the spiritual battles we face.*

LIVE IT OUT

What will you do this week to trust in Christ and rely on what He has provided? Consider the following suggestions:

▶ **Pray.** Take everything to God in prayer. Everything. Your victories begin with prayer. Make prayer a regular part of your day, knowing you need to continually look to God for strength.

▶ **Stand.** If you find you're susceptible to "the flaming arrows of the evil one"—his lies, doubts, and temptations—use God's armor. Identify several promises from God's Word on which you can stand against spiritual attacks.

▶ **Stand together.** Meet with someone you trust this week to talk about mutual accountability. Discuss ways to support and encourage each other in the spiritual battles you face.

Don't lose sight of the fact you're in a spiritual battle that doesn't include just you. You have help! You have the support of your friends and family. More importantly, you have the support of God, who empowers you to stand.

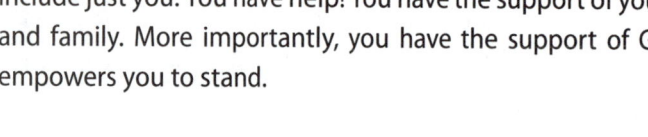

Share with others how you will live out this study: **#BSFLdarkside**

6 | BATTLE PLAN

Where do you turn when you need a fool-proof plan?

QUESTION #1

#BSFLdarkside

BIBLE STUDIES FOR LIFE **47**

THE POINT

We can follow Jesus' example in defeating spiritual attacks.

THE BIBLE MEETS LIFE

On October 8, 1871, a fire broke out in Chicago that killed an estimated 300 people, left 100,000 others homeless, and destroyed over 17,000 buildings. Over the years, Mrs. O'Leary's cow took the heat (no pun intended) for the Great Chicago Fire, but historians eventually removed the blame from this poor animal.

One good thing came out of this tragedy: people became more aware of the need for fire safety. Since 1922, America has commemorated the date of the Great Chicago Fire by observing a National Fire Prevention Week. Schools perform fire drills with their students, and firefighters encourage families to identify ways to prevent fires and establish plans for what to do when a fire does occur.

We face the threat of fire in another way. Satan, our enemy, seeks to harm us with "the flaming arrows of the evil one" (Eph. 6:16). He continually seeks to tempt us and pull us away from God's gracious and loving desire for our lives. Satan may be crafty, but our Lord is greater, and He modeled for us a foolproof plan to avoid getting burned by spiritual attacks.

WHAT DOES THE BIBLE SAY?

Matthew 4:1-4

[1] Then Jesus was led up by the Spirit into the wilderness to be tempted by the devil. [2] After he had fasted forty days and forty nights, he was hungry. [3] Then the tempter approached him and said, "If you are the Son of God, tell these stones to become bread." [4] He answered, "It is written: Man must not live on bread alone but on every word that comes from the mouth of God."

None of us is immune to temptation. For some of us, certain things continually tempt us. When we read of the temptations Jesus faced, we might be inclined to assume temptation wasn't a struggle for Him because, after all, He's God! Surely He didn't face the temptations we face today.

Think again. Jesus is God, but He's also fully man. And although He didn't face the exact same temptations we faced last week, He faced the same *types* of temptations. The writer of Hebrews had this to say about Jesus: "For we do not have a high priest who is unable to sympathize with our weaknesses, but one who has been tempted in every way as we are, yet without sin" (Heb. 4:15).

Satan came against Jesus with three temptations. The first temptation centered on Jesus' physical needs. The purpose of fasting is to focus on God through intense prayer. So, Jesus had been feeding Himself spiritually in prayer and communion with His Father. Yet He was likely weak on a physical level, since he had not eaten in 40 days. Satan attempted to exploit this weakness.

"If you are the Son of God" carries the force of jeering—as if to say, *"Why not use your power as God to meet a legitimate need in Your own life?"* The temptation was for Jesus to misuse, even exploit, His Messianic power for personal gain. Jesus insisted He would not act according to His own will, but only the will of the Father. (See John 6:38.) Therefore, Jesus would trust the provision of His Father instead of taking action for self-gratification.

> **What are some ways we face temptation through our physical appetites?**
>
> QUESTION #2

| THE POINT | We can follow Jesus' example in defeating spiritual attacks. |

Jesus responded to Satan by quoting from the Book of Deuteronomy: "It is written: Man must not live on bread alone but on every word that comes from the mouth of God." Jesus would live in obedience to the Word of God and nothing else. No matter how physically hungry He may have been at the moment, He would maintain His trust in a loving Father who would provide what He needed.

Matthew 4:5-7

⁵ Then the devil took him to the holy city, had him stand on the pinnacle of the temple, ⁶ and said to him, "If you are the Son of God, throw yourself down. For it is written: He will give his angels orders concerning you, and they will support you with their hands so that you will not strike your foot against a stone." ⁷ Jesus told him, "It is also written: Do not test the Lord your God."

Satan is cunning. Since Jesus deflected the first attack by reminding the devil that we live in obedience to every word of God, Satan's next attempt involved using Scripture as part of his temptation.

Before he quoted Scripture, Satan took Jesus to Jerusalem and "had him stand on the pinnacle of the temple." The temple represented God's presence and power to the Jewish people. Therefore, if Jesus jumped from this highest point, He could demonstrate God's power because, as Satan quoted from Psalm 91:11-12, "He will give his angels orders concerning you, and they will support you with their hands so that you will not strike your foot against a stone."

There's a big problem with that: Satan was taking the passage out of context. Satan used a psalm centered on God's care and protection for us when difficulties arise, then tried to justify putting God to the test. Instead of rightfully treating the passage as an acknowledgment of God's protection when harm comes, Satan tried to make a case for Jesus deliberately putting Himself in harm's way.

PROMISES, PROMISES

Use the space below to record promises we often encounter in our culture—promises from advertisements, from entertainment, from politicians, and so on. Add as many promises as you can think of in a few minutes.

What's one step you can take to get better at using Scripture to evaluate these promises?

"Jesus refused to exchange the end-time exaltation by the Father for a right-now exaltation of a snake."

—RUSSELL MOORE

| THE POINT | *We can follow Jesus' example in defeating spiritual attacks.* |

We're often tempted to challenge God, as well. The Israelites did that when they needed water in the wilderness. Instead of praying and looking to God for provision, they questioned and doubted His plan. They put God to the test. Years later, Moses reminded the people of this incident. (See Deut. 6:16.) Now, as He stood before a Scripture-twisting tempter, Jesus repeated the same command God taught His people through Moses: "Do not test the Lord your God."

When we're tempted to question God, doubt Him, or put Him to the test, we can stand strong by doing the following:

> **Know what God's Word says.** We should always read a Bible verse or passage in its correct context. Scripture interprets Scripture. Jesus would not let Satan twist a passage of Scripture for his own agenda, and neither should we. Psalm 91 needs to be understood in light of Deuteronomy 6. The Bible corroborates the Bible. The more we immerse ourselves in Scripture—all of Scripture—the better we become at detecting Satan's lies.

> **Rest in God's love and security.** Jesus knew the truth of Psalm 91:11-12, which is that God does protect and care for us; God gives us no reason to question that or test its truthfulness. We can always trust God regardless of what may tempt us to think otherwise. God loves us completely, and nothing will separate us from His love and protection. "What then are we to say about these things? If God is for us, who is against us?" (Rom. 8:31; see also vv. 32-39.)

What are some ways we are tempted to test God?

QUESTION #3

Matthew 4:8-10

8 Again, the devil took him to a very high mountain and showed him all the kingdoms of the world and their splendor. 9 And he said to him, "I will give you all these things if you will fall down and worship me." 10 Then Jesus told him, "Go away, Satan! For it is written: Worship the Lord your God, and serve only him."

Finally, Satan offered his boldest temptation. He took Jesus "to a very high mountain and showed him all the kingdoms of the world and their splendor." Satan could offer those kingdoms legitimately, since even Jesus acknowledged him as "the ruler of this world" (John 12:31; 14:30; 16:11). But why would Jesus even consider such an offer? After all, Jesus knew God's plan. Jesus knew He would ultimately gain all these kingdoms and rule them forever.

One thing made Satan's offer attractive. Jesus also knew that the road He was about to travel would include pain, suffering, and death. Jesus could avoid all that if He accepted Satan's offer. It would mean the instant achievement of His goal without any of the suffering.

We face the same type of temptation today. We want success, pleasure, possessions—things that are not wrong in and of themselves, but are wrong when we take shortcuts to achieve them. But the temptation to take such shortcuts always comes with a catch, and Satan's offer to Jesus was no different. "I will give you all these things if you will fall down and worship me."

Jesus had enough. "Go away, Satan! For it is written: Worship the Lord your God, and serve only him."

Pride will lead us down the enemy's short path to success, happiness, or whatever we're chasing—but the price we pay will destroy us. On the other hand, humility before God will ultimately lead us to experience far more than we can imagine. When tempted to take the shortcut and compromise our worship of God, we should remember God's promises: "What no eye has seen, no ear has heard, and no human heart has conceived—God has prepared these things for those who love him" (1 Cor. 2:9).

> *What are we often tempted to worship in place of God?*
>
> QUESTION #4

> *What can we learn from Jesus' example about overcoming spiritual attacks?*
>
> QUESTION #5

BIBLE STUDIES FOR LIFE

| THE POINT | We can follow Jesus' example in defeating spiritual attacks. |

LIVE IT OUT

Based on our study this week, what steps will you take to defeat the attacks that come your way? Consider these suggestions:

- ▶ **Look to Jesus.** Be intentional about keeping your focus on Christ. Lean on Him for strength to stand, knowing He understands. "For since he himself has suffered when he was tempted, he is able to help those who are tempted" (Heb. 2:18).

- ▶ **Stay clear.** If you know of people, places, or circumstances that fuel your vulnerability to temptation and spiritual attack, resolve to avoid those things. For best results, talk to someone else about your decision.

- ▶ **Memorize Scripture.** Make Scripture memory a weekly discipline and habit. Begin with memorizing verses that address areas where you often feel tempted or under attack.

Expect opposition when you step forward in faith. Spiritual attacks will come. But we can follow Jesus' example to stand against those attacks and remain victorious.

My thoughts

Share with others how you will live out this study: #BSFLdarkside

UNITED IN PRAYER

BY STEPHEN KENDRICK AND ALEX KENDRICK,
WITH TRAVIS AGNEW

When an army of people work together to accomplish a goal, it becomes a formidable force indeed.

An interesting passage in Genesis 11 describes the construction of the tower of Babel. In this biblical account, ungodly people decided to build a city with an enormous tower for their own glory and prestige. They planned it out and began the challenge, and at first found success in their efforts.

But God looked down from heaven and basically said, "Because of their unity, nothing will be impossible for them." (See v. 6.) So He intervened.

God divided them by changing their communication into numerous languages to prevent them from finishing their prideful monument. In the confusion and chaos, they abandoned the project and separated themselves by language, spreading out across the land.

What is so striking about this passage of Scripture is that God Himself noted that when people are unified, they're able to exert tremendous power and momentum. Even ungodly people! So imagine how powerful unity can be for people who worship and obey the God of the universe.

If they seek the Lord and act in unity, nothing can stop them.

> *Imagine how powerful unity can be for people who worship and obey the God of the universe.*

That's why the enemy does everything possible to keep God's people divided. Because once we come together in unity, we gain momentum and ground for the kingdom. United prayer is powerful. But prayer from a divided people—well, not so much. This is why removing bitterness toward others and choosing to forgive is so crucial. In fact, any pride or selfishness should be seen as an enemy of unified prayer.

In John 17, Jesus prayed a beautiful prayer, asking God to unify believers into one body, that the world would know He was sent by God to bring salvation to the world. (See v. 21.) Psalm 133:1 echoes the same theme: "How good and pleasant it is when brothers live together in harmony!"

God loves and blesses unity. It speaks volumes about the body of Christ when we worship together and love one another as God intended. It also draws attention to our Savior, who died to cleanse our sins and now lives to intercede for us to God the Father.

When people see unity, they see purpose, love, and power. It's attractive and beautiful. And when an army of people work together to accomplish a goal, it becomes a formidable force indeed.

John 13:34-35 says: "I give you a new command: Love one another. Just as I have loved you, you are also to love one another. By this everyone will know that you are my disciples, if you love one another."

Jesus' words here are clear, and the model Jesus gave us through His life and ministry makes it even more clear—we're to love our neighbor. And our neighbor is anyone and everyone who is a part of our lives.

So, before we can tackle this concept of prayer in a serious way, we need to not only evaluate our relationship with God, but also our relationship with others.

Stephen Kendrick is a cowriter and producer of the movies *WAR ROOM, Courageous, Facing the Giants,* and *Fireproof.* He is cowriter with Alex Kendrick of the *New York Times* bestsellers *The Resolution for Men* and *The Love Dare.*

Alex Kendrick is best known as an actor, writer, and director of the films *Fireproof, Courageous, Facing the Giants,* and *WAR ROOM.* He is coauthor of four *New York Times* bestselling books.

Travis Agnew is Family & Worship Pastor at North Side Baptist Church in Greenwood, SC. He also serves as adjunct religion instructor at Lander University.

LEADER GUIDE — THE DARK SIDE

GENERAL INSTRUCTIONS

In order to make the most of this study and to ensure a richer group experience, it's recommended that all group participants read through the teaching and discussion content in full before each group meeting. As a leader, it is also a good idea for you to be familiar with this content and prepared to summarize it for your group members as you move through the material each week.

Each session of the Bible study is made up of three sections:

1. THE BIBLE MEETS LIFE.

An introduction to the theme of the session and its connection to everyday life, along with a brief overview of the primary Scripture text. This section also includes an icebreaker question or activity.

2. WHAT DOES THE BIBLE SAY?

This comprises the bulk of each session and includes the primary Scripture text along with explanations for key words and ideas within that text. This section also includes most of the content designed to produce and maintain discussion within the group.

3. LIVE IT OUT.

The final section focuses on application, using bulleted summary statements to answer the question, *So what?* As the leader, be prepared to challenge the group to apply what they learned during the discussion by transforming it into action throughout the week.

The Dark Side Leader Guide contains several features and tools designed to help you lead participants through the material provided.

QUESTION 1—ICEBREAKER

These opening questions and/or activities are designed to help participants transition into the study and begin engaging the primary themes to be discussed. Be sure everyone has a chance to speak, but maintain a low-pressure environment.

DISCUSSION QUESTIONS

Each "What Does the Bible Say?" section features six questions designed to spark discussion and interaction within your group. These questions encourage critical thinking, so be sure to allow a period of silence for participants to process the question and form an answer.

The Dark Side Leader Guide also contains follow-up questions and optional activities that may be helpful to your group, if time permits.

DVD CONTENT

Each video features Jeremiah Johnston discussing the primary themes found in the session. We recommend you show this video in one of three places: 1) At the beginning of the group time, 2) After the icebreaker, or 3) After a quick review and/or summary of "What Does the Bible Say?" A video summary is included as well. You may choose to use this summary as background preparation to help you guide the group.

The Leader Guide contains additional questions to help unpack the video and transition into the discussion. For a digital Leader Guide with commentary, see the "Leader Tools" folder on the DVD-ROM in your Leader Kit.

For helps on how to use *Bible Studies for Life,* tips on how to better lead groups, or additional ideas for leading, visit: *ministrygrid.com/web/BibleStudiesforLife.*

SESSION 1: SATAN

The Point: Satan fights against us, but we can stand in Christ.

The Passage: Revelation 12:7-12

The Setting: The apostle John wrote the Book of Revelation. John was exiled to the island of Patmos. While on the island, John received the revelation he recorded for us. (See Rev. 1:9-11.) His first-century readers included the seven churches in Asia (what is modern Asia Minor, v. 11). One of John's purposes was to encourage believers who faced persecution for their belief in Jesus.

QUESTION 1: What monster or fictional villain best represents evil to you?

Optional activity: Prior to the group gathering, print out several pictures showing how Satan has been represented in history and in our current culture. (Think red horns with a trident, as one example.) Pass these images around the group and encourage people to discuss these questions: 1) What do these images communicate about Satan? 2) How do these images compare and contrast with a biblical view of Satan?

Note: Be sure to use restraint when selecting images to show your group members. Avoid pictures that would be offensive or unnecessarily unsettling.

Video Summary: The Scripture teaches that there is a very real demonic force. His name is Satan. He's been cast out of heaven and utterly defeated through the death, burial, and resurrection of Jesus Christ. As Christians, we do not need to live in fear of Satan. He does not have power over us. Satan is not omniscient. Satan is not omnipresent. Satan is not all-powerful. Only God is.

▶ WATCH THE DVD SEGMENT FOR SESSION 1. THEN USE THE FOLLOWING QUESTIONS AND DISCUSSION POINTS TO TRANSITION INTO THE STUDY.

- Based on your personal experience, what words would you use to describe Satan?
- When has the enemy deceived you? What lies did you believe?

WHAT DOES THE BIBLE SAY?

▶ ASK FOR A VOLUNTEER TO READ ALOUD REVELATION 12:7-12.

Response: What's your initial reaction to these verses?

- What do you like about the text?
- What questions do you have about these verses?

▶ TURN THE GROUP'S ATTENTION TO REVELATION 12:7-9.

QUESTION 2: What have you been taught about the devil?

In most cases, this will not be the appropriate time to correct what group members have been taught. Allow them to express what they've heard, and then use the remainder of this session to teach truth.

> ***Optional follow-up:*** In what areas of life are we most susceptible to Satan's lies?

QUESTION 3: Where do you see evidence of Satan's deceptive work in the world today?

This question will give group members an opportunity to identify where and how they see evidence of Satan in their daily lives, community, and the world. Encourage them to share personal stories as well as things they have witnessed in the media or though other channels.

▶ MOVE TO REVELATION 12:10.

QUESTION 4: How should we understand Satan's role as our "accuser"?

This question calls for application based on the biblical text and is designed to help group members better grasp how Satan works as our accuser. Encourage them to listen to and learn from each other.

> ***Optional activity:*** Direct group members to complete the activity "Not Even Close" on page 11. If time permits, encourage volunteers to share how they would like to see the church better communicate God's superiority over Satan.

> ***Optional follow-up:*** How would you compare the Messiah and the accuser as described in this verse?

▶ CONTINUE WITH REVELATION 12:11-12.

QUESTION 5: What are some ways we can defend against Satan's accusations?

Encourage group members to work together and brainstorm specific ways they can defend against Satan's accusations. This promotes group connection as members work together on a plan to act on biblical principles.

> ***Optional follow-up:*** How should these verses shape our lives each day?

Note: The following question does not appear in the group member book. Use it in your group discussion as time allows.

QUESTION 6: What does this passage tell us about our battle against the enemy?

Answering this question requires group members to examine the biblical text to learn what they need to know personally regarding their battle against the enemy.

> ***Optional follow-up:*** How would you respond to people who tell you they don't believe in Satan?

BIBLE STUDIES FOR LIFE

LIVE IT OUT

We can overcome Satan through Jesus. Encourage group members to consider the following suggestions of ways they can walk in that victory this week:

- **Confess.** Turn from sin and give Satan no grounds for accusations in your life. Place your trust in Christ for forgiveness and freedom.

- **Read.** Make Scripture reading a daily habit. Let the truth of Scripture fill your mind rather than the deceit and lies of Satan. Test every thought to see how it stands against the truth of Christ in His Word.

- **Speak.** When you see others living in false guilt and believing the lies of Satan, point to the victory they can have in Christ. Lead them to embrace the truth and walk in victory.

Challenge: Don't fall into the trap of believing evil doesn't exist—or believing that evil only impacts the world in faraway places. Satan is a clear and present danger to God's people. Thankfully, our status as God's people means we can claim the victory He has already won. Be on the lookout this week for opportunities to intentionally claim that victory.

Pray: Ask for prayer requests and ask group members to pray for the different requests as intercessors. As the leader, conclude by affirming the truth that Jesus has already gained victory over Satan. Declare that truth. Ask for God's Spirit to remind you of that truth each day as you walk with Him.

SESSION 2: DEMONS

The Point: Demonic forces are real, but Christ is greater.

The Passage: Mark 9:17-29

The Setting: Jesus had taken Peter, James, and John up a high mountain, where they witnessed Jesus' transfiguration. (See Mark 9:2-8.) In their absence, a man brought his son to the other nine disciples, hoping they would be able to drive out a spirit possessing his son. When Jesus and the three disciples returned, they found a group of scribes disputing with the other disciples over the disciples' failure to drive the spirit out of the boy.

QUESTION 1: What do you typically do when you feel afraid?

To be more specific, you are asking what your group members typically do to shake off or process their feelings of fear. Do they hide? Do they try to distract themselves? Do they confront what's making them afraid? And so on.

> ***Optional activity:*** *The Screwtape Letters*, written by C. S. Lewis, is a fictional collection of letters written from an experienced demon to his less-experienced nephew. The book is written from a Christian worldview, yet each letter offers advice and strategies for the temptation and corruption of a human "patient"—making the book an interesting exploration of demonic activity. Read one of these letters to your group to help them connect with the reality of spiritual warfare, along with the need to actively stand against evil.
>
> **Note:** The complete text for *The Screwtape Letters* is available online, and you can find a link at our blog: biblestudiesforlife.com/adultextra.

Video Summary: This week's text is the only place in the Gospels where the disciples are unable to cast out the demon. The word *demons* is used 63 times in the Gospels. It's something Jesus talked about all the time. And it's something we need to know about as believers—specifically, what the Word has to say about demons. When we invite Jesus into any situation where there is demonic activity, the game changes.

▶ WATCH THE DVD SEGMENT FOR SESSION 2. THEN USE THE FOLLOWING QUESTIONS AND DISCUSSION POINTS TO TRANSITION INTO THE STUDY.

- How are you bringing God into situations where there is a spiritual stronghold?
- When has unbelief affected your ability to invite Jesus into such a situation?

WHAT DOES THE BIBLE SAY?

▶ ASK FOR A VOLUNTEER TO READ ALOUD MARK 9:17-29.

Response: What's your initial reaction to these verses?

- What questions do you have about these verses?
- What do you hope to learn this week about being more aware of demonic forces?

▶ TURN THE GROUP'S ATTENTION TO MARK 9:17-22A.

QUESTION 2: What have you been taught about demons and demon possession?

As in the previous session, allow people to speak freely, and then rely on God's Word and the remainder of this study to replace any false teachings with biblical truth.

▶ MOVE TO MARK 9:22B-27.

QUESTION 3: What strikes you as most interesting about these verses? Why?

This question is designed to help group members actively engage the Scripture text and then share in their own words what speaks most powerfully to them in these verses.

Optional follow-up: What are some obstacles that cause us to struggle with our faith?

QUESTION 4: When have you felt like the father in these verses—wanting to believe but struggling to do so?

Identifying emotions and feelings in a person's life journey is important in moving them to better understand God. Questions like this also help us better understand what it is we truly believe about God and how those beliefs manifest themselves in our lives.

Optional activity: Direct group members to complete the activity "Personal Assessment: Prayer" on page 21.

▶ CONTINUE WITH MARK 9:28-29.

QUESTION 5: Why is faith in Jesus essential when dealing with evil?

We all deal with evil. Identifying what is essential in fighting that battle is the first step in gaining confidence that we're equipped for the fight and ready to move forward in the truth that God is the only one who can bring victory over evil.

Optional follow-up: What are the practical differences between trying to fight evil versus allowing Jesus to fight evil for us?

Note: The following question does not appear in the group member book. Use it in your group discussion as time allows.

QUESTION 6: How do fasting and prayer prepare us for spiritual warfare?

This questions gives group members an opportunity to examine some actions that can help prepare them for spiritual warfare as well as the difference these actions can make. Encourage them to be specific in their answers.

Optional follow-up: When have you felt God's strength and support after a time of fasting and/or prayer?

LIVE IT OUT

What steps can you take to ground yourself in Christ as preparation for the enemy's attacks this week? Invite group members to consider these suggestions:

- **Pray often.** Ask God to increase and strengthen your faith. Make it a habit to ask God to strengthen your faith and guide you into a deeper truth in Him.

- **Pray daily.** Stop relying on yourself as you face difficulties and spiritual attacks. Express your total dependence on God through prayer at the beginning of each day.

- **Pray constantly.** Invite the presence of Jesus into every situation. Form the discipline of continually conversing with God's Spirit as you encounter new situations and circumstances throughout each day.

Challenge: In this passage from Mark 9, we see that the demon's work in the boy's life dominated the crowd, the disciples, the father, and his son—until Jesus showed up. What difference could it make in your life this week if you live empowered by the truth that He has all authority and all power no matter the spiritual attack you are under?

Pray: Ask for prayer requests and ask group members to pray for the different requests as intercessors. As the leader, conclude by proclaiming your belief that Christ is greater than any and all forces of evil. Stake your claim as His disciple in the fight against darkness, and pray that your group members will do the same.

SESSION 3: THE PARANORMAL

The Point: Dabbling with evil is destructive; seeking direction from God brings life.

The Passage: Deuteronomy 18:9-18

The Setting: The Israelites lived in a world that embraced occult practices. The Egyptian Pharaoh, for instance, had magicians to advise him. (See Gen. 41:8.) When Moses confronted the Pharaoh, the Pharaoh summoned the "wise men and sorcerers—the magicians of Egypt" who did their "occult practices" (Ex. 7:11). Occult practices were widespread in the promised land of Canaan as well. God instructed the Israelites, His covenant people, that they were to completely reject these practices.

QUESTION 1: What movies or TV shows bank on our culture's interest in the paranormal?

These can be movies and shows from the past or ones that are currently popular in the culture.

> *Optional activity:* Bring several copies of newspapers and/or magazines to your group gathering. Pass out one copy to each group member, and ask them to look for stories, advertisements, articles, and so on that may encourage readers to dabble in the paranormal—items that promote or encourage a non-biblical view of the supernatural. Encourage volunteers to share what they find as long as those finds are appropriate for your specific setting.
>
> **Note:** If you're not able to collect magazines and newspapers, you can ask group members to use their smartphones to look through popular websites, and explore news websites in search of offers or advertisements that dabble in the paranormal.

Video Summary: The paranormal is so commonplace in our society many people don't even see it as dangerous. We need to avoid any kind of contact with the paranormal world around us. The Bible does not present such practices as harmless, because they encourage us to seek guidance apart from God. Truth is found in God, and He gives us all the direction we need.

▶ WATCH THE DVD SEGMENT FOR SESSION 3. THEN USE THE FOLLOWING QUESTIONS AND DISCUSSION POINTS TO TRANSITION INTO THE STUDY.

- How would you define *paranormal*?
- Have you ever had an experience you would consider paranormal? Explain.

WHAT DOES THE BIBLE SAY?

▶ ASK FOR A VOLUNTEER TO READ ALOUD DEUTERONOMY 18:9-18.

Response: What's your initial reaction to these verses?

- What questions do you have about these verses?
- What new application do you hope to get from this passage?

▶ TURN THE GROUP'S ATTENTION TO DEUTERONOMY 18:9-11.

QUESTION 2: What have you been taught about the practices mentioned in these verses?

There are no right or wrong answers to this question. It is designed to give group members an opportunity to identify and examine what they have come to believe about the biblical text based on what they have been taught by family members, friends, and other influences in their lives.

Optional follow-up: When have you come face to face with one of the practices mentioned in these verses?

QUESTION 3: Why do people still dabble in these kinds of practices?

Encourage them to go beyond the surface-level answers to this question. Instead, ask group members to engage and identify the core motivations that drive people to occultic practices. What are they looking for? What are they hoping to achieve?

Optional follow-up: What evidence do you see that our culture is fascinated with the paranormal and the occult?

▶ MOVE TO DEUTERONOMY 18:12-14.

QUESTION 4: What makes paranormal practices so dangerous and destructive?

Let group members spend some time discussing this question as a group rather then individually. Encourage them to listen closely to the input of other group members. Much can be learned from each other in community.

Optional activity: Direct group members to complete the activity "What Would You Say?" on page 28. If time permits, encourage volunteers to share their responses.

▶ CONTINUE WITH DEUTERONOMY 18:15-18.

QUESTION 5: What are reliable ways for us to seek out God's plan and purpose in our lives?

This is an application question included to encourage group members to share action steps based on what they have learned from the biblical text.

Note: The following question does not appear in the group member book. Use it in your group discussion as time allows.

QUESTION 6: What are some ways we can communicate truth to others about the paranormal and psychic practices?

This question provides group members with an opportunity to identify practical steps toward positive action. Try to steer them away from talking theory; encourage them to get practical.

Optional follow-up: What are some ways Christians water down or ignore the dangers of the paranormal?

LIVE IT OUT

What steps can you take this week to shine the light of Jesus against the darkness of the paranormal? Encourage group members to consider these suggestions to get started:

- **Be educated.** You will only know God's guidance as you immerse yourself in His Word. Commit to reading the Bible on a daily basis and develop the practice of studying its truth.

- **Be discerning.** Make discernment a regular part of your prayer life. Ask God to guide your thoughts and actions away from evil. "But test all things. Hold on to what is good. Stay away from every kind of evil" (1 Thess. 5:21-22).

- **Be blameless.** Seek to demonstrate a blameless heart, fully devoted to the Lord, by removing from your presence anything that promotes and encourages the use of paranormal practices. Make a line in the sand.

Challenge: People in our culture are fascinated with the paranormal because they are longing for God. Choose the path of light over darkness—not only for yourself, but for those who need to see Christ. Spend this week watching for ways you can show the path of light to those who need to know God.

Pray: Ask for prayer requests and ask group members to pray for the different requests as intercessors. As the leader, conclude by affirming your desire to obey God regarding paranormal practices and other forms of the occult. Pray for clarity each day to see what is harmful in the world, and then to reject those practices.

SESSION 4: FEAR NOT!

The Point: We don't need to fear evil forces when we're in Christ.

The Passage: 1 John 4:1-6

The Setting: The apostle John wrote the Book of 1 John to a church in which false teachers were advocating a view of Christianity different from that of the apostles. These false teachers eventually left the church, but lingering doubts remained among members of the early church as to the nature of true Christian beliefs and practices. John wrote his letter in order to deal with these false teachers and to replace their heretical teachings with truth.

QUESTION 1: What are some of the most unusual phobias you've heard about?

Optional activity: Supplement Question 1 by asking group members to give their best guess on what people are afraid of when they suffer from the following phobias. Be sure to applaud anyone who gets one correct!

- **Arachnophobia:** the fear of spiders.
- **Heliophobia:** the fear of the sun, sunlight, or any bright light.
- **Arachibutyrophobia:** the fear of peanut butter sticking to the roof of the mouth.
- **Ergophobia:** an abnormal and persistent fear of work or finding employment.
- **Philophobia:** the irrational fear of falling in love or emotional relationships.
- **Pogonophobia:** the extreme dislike or fear of beards.

Video Summary: We have nothing to fear. The ultimate victory has been assured for us in Christ. And we are active participants in that victory. Evil is all around us. Evil can even present itself as good. We need discernment. We can recognize evil for what it is because the truth will always line up with Jesus Christ. We have a faith that is based on evidence.

▶ WATCH THE DVD SEGMENT FOR SESSION 4. THEN USE THE FOLLOWING QUESTIONS AND DISCUSSION POINTS TO TRANSITION INTO THE STUDY.

- In what ways has fear affected your discernment? Be specific.
- What does it mean to you to own your faith?

WHAT DOES THE BIBLE SAY?

▶ ASK FOR A VOLUNTEER TO READ ALOUD 1 JOHN 4:1-6.

Response: What's your initial reaction to these verses?

- What do you like about the text?
- What new application do you hope to receive about how to handle feeling fearful?

▶ TURN THE GROUP'S ATTENTION TO 1 JOHN 4:1-3.

QUESTION 2: Who comes to mind when you hear the word "discernment"? Why?

"Discernment" isn't a word most people use every day, so it may take some time for group members to process their thoughts and come up with an answer. You can still encourage group members to share their first reaction, but that reaction may not happen quickly.

Optional follow-up: What type of damage can be caused by false prophets and false teaching?

QUESTION 3: What are some distortions of the nature of Jesus we still hear today?

Encourage group members to skim through the bullet list at the bottom of page 34 to jump-start their thinking on how other religious systems view Jesus. However, be sure to mention that distortions about Jesus also come from sources outside of other religions.

Optional follow-up: What practical steps can you take to discern between false teaching and God's truth?

▶ MOVE TO 1 JOHN 4:4-6.

QUESTION 4: What emotions do you experience when you read this passage?

Group members sometimes need encouragement to share on a more personal level. If the question feels too broad, you can guide them in their discussion by asking more specific questions like: How does it make you feel to know as a member of God's family you are secure? What does it mean to you to know that in Christ you truly have nothing to fear?

Optional follow-up: How would you describe the two opposing spirits in the world today?

QUESTION 5: Jesus is greater than those who oppose us. How will this truth influence your life today and in the days to come?

This question requires that group members revisit the biblical text in order to move toward life application.

Optional activity: Encourage group members to complete the activity "Always" on page 35.

Note: The following question does not appear in the group member book. Use it in your group discussion as time allows.

QUESTION 6: How does this passage equip us to deal with the reality of evil in the world?

This question is designed to give groups members an opportunity to connect the biblical text with what it looks like to live out those truths in their everyday lives. Encourage them to be specific and practical in their answers.

BIBLE STUDIES FOR LIFE **69**

LIVE IT OUT

How will the truth that you have nothing to fear in Christ make a difference in your life? Invited group members to consider the following suggestions:

- **Memorize.** If you are prone to fear, memorize 1 John 4:4. Place cards with this verse in various places where you will see them throughout the day. Recite it whenever you feel afraid.

- **Be filled.** God has placed His Holy Spirit in your life. Stay focused in prayer so that you can continually rely on that Spirit to fill you, lead you, and give you discernment.

- **Be discerning.** Regularly evaluate the different "voices" you encounter in books, sermons, studies, online devotions, and articles. Determine what they believe about Christ and to what degree they lift up and honor the name of Christ.

Challenge: Severe phobias aren't the only factor that keeps us from experiencing the life we were meant to live. Yes, evil is real. But so is God—and He is far superior to any force or opposition that might move against us. Spend some time developing specific actions steps you will take this week when you start to feel afraid. Also consider how you can use those steps to help others who may be feeling fearful.

Pray: Ask for prayer requests and ask group members to pray for the different requests as intercessors. As the leader, conclude by echoing the truth from Scripture that God's Spirit is greater than any other force present in creation. Pray that you and your group members would rely on God's Spirit as you seek to serve Him each day.

SESSION 5: BATTLE ARMOR

The Point: God equips us for the spiritual battles we face.

The Passage: Ephesians 6:10-20

The Setting: Paul's letter to the church in Ephesus, most likely written around A.D. 60-61 during an imprisonment in Rome, is one of four letters called "Prison" or "Captivity" letters (including Philippians, Colossians, and Philemon). Paul briefly noted his imprisonment in this letter. (See Eph. 3:1; 4:1; 6:20.) A key topic in this letter is the spiritual armor we need to fight our spiritual battles.

QUESTION 1: What are some "tools of the trade" you rely on most days?

> *Optional activity:* Play a video clip from the *MacGyver* TV show. Choose a clip that shows MacGyver escaping from trouble using an especially strange or mundane set of tools. (An example video clip will be posted on the Leader Extra! blog at *biblestudiesforlife.com/adultextra*.) If time permits, make additional use of the clip by asking group members to think through other methods MacGyver could have used to escape.
>
> **Note:** If you're not in a position to play a video clip, or if you're not inclined to do so, bring in several examples of "tools of the trade." For example, bring a hammer, a calculator, a keyboard, a thermometer, and so on. Pass these around as object lessons while your group discusses Question 1.

Video Summary: Satan does not like it when we choose to follow and obey Christ. The great enemy of God will seek to pull us from full devotion to Him. Thankfully, we are not left alone to face this enemy. God will give us victory, but it doesn't happen automatically. We have to put on the full armor—weapons available to all Christians. As His children, God equips us with everything we need to stand against Satan.

▶ **WATCH THE DVD SEGMENT FOR SESSION 5. THEN USE THE FOLLOWING QUESTIONS AND DISCUSSION POINTS TO TRANSITION INTO THE STUDY.**

- In his video message, Jeremiah says, "We're either moving toward God or away from Him, living for Him or not living for Him. There is no middle ground." Spend some time thinking about where you fall right now. If you are comfortable, share your thoughts with your group.

WHAT DOES THE BIBLE SAY?

▶ **ASK FOR A VOLUNTEER TO READ ALOUD EPHESIANS 6:10-20.**

Response: What's your initial reaction to these verses?

- What questions do you have about these verses?
- What new application do you hope to get from this passage?

▶ **TURN THE GROUP'S ATTENTION TO EPHESIANS 6:10-13.**

QUESTION 2: What have you been taught about spiritual warfare?

As in previous sessions, this will not be the appropriate time to correct what group members have been taught. Encourage them to answer based on their experience and then use the remainder of this session to teach truth.

Optional follow-up: Where do you see evidence of spiritual attacks in today's world?

▶ **MOVE TO EPHESIANS 6:14-17.**

QUESTION 3: Which piece of God's armor most resonates with you? Why?

This question invites members of the group to share their personal testimonies based on past experience and/or current need. Encourage them to be honest.

Optional follow-up: How does this armor help you face a spiritual battle?

QUESTION 4: What are some real-life situations in which this armor is essential for followers of Christ?

If possible, encourage group members to share a little of their stories as they engage this question. Ask if they would be willing to describe real-life situations in which they have depended on God's armor in a practical way—or situations where they wished they would have done so. Allowing people to open up and share their experiences is a great way to learn and build unity within the group at the same time.

Optional follow-up: Who in your life wears this armor well and knows how to use it?

Optional activity: Direct group members to complete the activity "Standing Firm" on page 45. If time permits, encourage volunteers to share their responses.

▶ **CONTINUE WITH EPHESIANS 6:18-20.**

QUESTION 5: How does prayer contribute to our efforts in spiritual warfare?

This is another opportunity to encourage group members to share their own experiences. How have they seen prayer contribute to their spiritual lives? Their efforts in spiritual warfare?

Optional follow-up: How can we help one another be more active and intentional in prayer?

Note: The following question does not appear in the group member book. Use it in your group discussion as time allows.

QUESTION 6: What keeps us from actively engaging in spiritual warfare?

Answering this question requires group members to examine the things in their own lives that have kept them from actively engaging. Remind them that they aren't alone as you encourage their honesty.

Optional follow-up: How can we help one another as we engage in spiritual warfare?

LIVE IT OUT

Encourage group members to consider these suggestions of things they can do this week to trust in Christ and rely on what He has provided:

- **Pray.** Take everything to God in prayer. Everything. Your victories begin with prayer. Make prayer a regular part of your day, knowing you need to continually look to God for strength.

- **Stand.** If you find you're susceptible to "the flaming arrows of the evil one"—his lies, doubts, and temptations—use God's armor. Identify several promises from God's Word on which you can stand against spiritual attacks.

- **Stand Together.** Meet with someone you trust this week to talk about mutual accountability. Discuss ways to support and encourage each other in the spiritual battles you face.

Challenge: Don't lose sight of the fact you are in a spiritual battle that does not include just you. You have help! You have the support of your friends and family. More importantly, you have the support of God, who empowers you to stand. Spend some time this week talking to your family and close friends. Ask them how you can best support them in their battle and share with them how they can best support you.

Pray: Ask for prayer requests and ask group members to pray for the different requests as intercessors. As the leader, conclude by thanking God for the gift of His armor—for making His armor available to you and to the members of your group. Pray for courage to use that armor in order to stand.

SESSION 6: BATTLE PLAN

The Point: We can follow Jesus' example in defeating spiritual attacks.

The Passage: Matthew 4:1-10

The Setting: After describing the events associated with Jesus' birth (see Matt. 1–2) and the ministry of John the Baptist (see 3:1-12), Matthew detailed how Jesus was baptized by John the Baptist, during which God affirmed Jesus as His Son (see vv. 13-17). Jesus was then led into the wilderness by the Holy Spirit, where He was tempted three times by the devil. This episode in the life of Jesus is mentioned in the Gospels of Matthew, Luke (see Luke 4:1-13), and Mark (see Mark 1:12-13).

QUESTION 1: Where do you turn when you need a fool-proof plan?

Remind group members that they are free to move beyond "spiritual" answers. What are some places in addition to God's Word where they look for a fool-proof plan?

> ***Optional activity:*** Bring a chess board and pieces to your group gathering as an object lesson of using strategy to defeat an enemy. Pass the pieces around to your group members while discussing Question 1.
>
> **Note:** You could also consider asking for two volunteers to play an actual game of chess while you and your group members discussion Question 1. If you choose this route, you can either set a time limit for the game or simply allow the volunteers to continue playing while the group moves forward with the session.

Video Summary: Everybody encounters temptation. Satan knows what to use in his attempts to get us to sin. We might assume that because a certain temptation feels unique to us, no one knows what we're going through. However, Jesus knows. He faced the same types of temptation we face. We can stand against temptation in the same way He did.

▶ WATCH THE DVD SEGMENT FOR SESSION 6. THEN USE THE FOLLOWING QUESTIONS AND DISCUSSION POINTS TO TRANSITION INTO THE STUDY.

- What steps will you take this week to make sure the devil doesn't know the Bible better than you?
- What battle plan do you have in place for the next time Satan tries to misdirect you? Be specific.

WHAT DOES THE BIBLE SAY?

▶ ASK FOR A VOLUNTEER TO READ ALOUD MATTHEW 4:1-10.

Response: What's your initial reaction to these verses?

- What questions do you have about preparing to stand against temptation?
- What new application do you hope to get from this passage?

▶ TURN THE GROUP'S ATTENTION TO MATTHEW 4:1-4.

QUESTION 2: What are some ways we face temptation through our physical appetites?

This question calls for application based on the biblical text and is designed to help group members identify what this looks like in their daily lives. Encourage them to be specific in their responses. Because this question is broad in scope, be prepared to start the discussion with some ideas of your own.

Optional follow-up: When have you felt especially nourished by God's Word?

▶ MOVE TO MATTHEW 4:5-7.

QUESTION 3: What are some ways we are tempted to test God?

Another way to phrase this question would be: "What are some ways we often try to force or trick God into doing what we want instead of submitting to what He wants?"

Optional follow-up: Why is it dangerous to test God?

▶ CONTINUE WITH MATTHEW 4:8-10.

QUESTION 4: What are we often tempted to worship in place of God?

Answering this question requires group members to examine the things they are tempted to worship in place of God. Encourage them to be honest and consider sharing an experience of your own.

Optional activity: Direct group members to complete the activity "Promises, Promises" on page 51. If time permits, ask volunteers to share their responses.

QUESTION 5: What can we learn from Jesus' example about overcoming spiritual attacks?

This question is designed to guide group members to life application based on the Scripture text. Encourage them to revisit the passage and then brainstorm responses in two phases: (1) What example did Jesus set? and (2) In what ways can we apply His example to our lives when we encounter spiritual attacks?

Optional follow-up: How can we prepare ourselves for the temptations that will come our way?

Note: The following question does not appear in the group member book. Use it in your group discussion as time allows.

QUESTION 6: How can we help one another in our struggle against temptation?

This question is designed to give group members an opportunity to discuss together and develop an intentional plan of action designed to provide accountability and help each other deal with temptation.

LIVE IT OUT

Based on your study this week, invite group members to consider what steps they will take to defeat the attacks that come their way:

- **Look to Jesus.** Be intentional about keeping your focus on Christ. Lean on Him for strength to stand, knowing He understands. "For since he himself has suffered when he was tempted, he is able to help those who are tempted" (Heb. 2:18).

- **Stay clear.** If you know of people, places, or circumstances that fuel your vulnerability to temptation and spiritual attack, resolve to avoid those things. For best results, talk to someone else about your decision.

- **Memorize Scripture.** Make Scripture memory a weekly discipline and habit. Begin with memorizing verses that address areas where you often feel tempted or under attack.

Challenge: Expect opposition when you step forward in faith. Spiritual attacks will come. In what ways can you follow Jesus' example to stand against those attacks and remain victorious this week?

Pray: As the leader, close this final session of *The Dark Side* in prayer. Thank God for the privilege of studying His Word throughout this resource. Conclude the study by praising God that we can rest in the truth that Satan has been defeated by Christ. There is a dark side, but the light of Christ has overcome the darkness.

Note: If you haven't discussed it yet, decide as a group whether or not you plan to continue to meet together and, if so, what Bible study options you would like to pursue. Visit *LifeWay.com/smallgroups* for help, or if you would like more studies like this one, visit *biblestudiesforlife.com/smallgroups*.

Join the Conversation

Bible Studies for Life is online!
There are lots of ways to interact with people around the world
who are going through the same Bible study as your group.

facebook.com/biblestudiesforlife
Interact with other group leaders and members. Ask questions. Share stories. Get helpful links to additional resources.

@biblemeetslife
Follow us to stay up to date with our latest blog articles and other *Bible Studies for Life* news. You can also respond to discussion questions by using hashtags that go along with each session, such as #BSFLpeace, or creating hashtags just for your group.

My group's prayer requests

My group's prayer requests

ALSO AVAILABLE ...

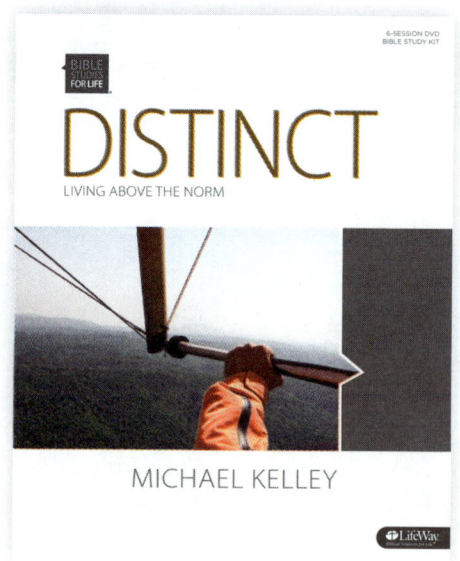

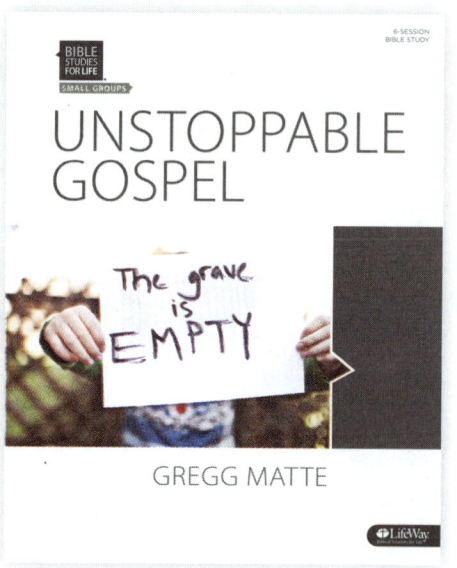

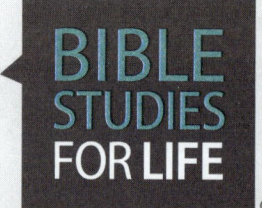

This series helps people understand how to apply the Bible to everyday life—their families, their careers, and their struggles—just as they are, right where they live. A new study releases every three months.

Discover available studies at **biblestudiesforlife.com/smallgroups**, **800.458.2772**, or at your **LifeWay Christian Store**.